Owls

Owls

Michael George
THE CHILD'S WORLD, INC.

Library of Congress Cataloging-in-Publication Data
George, Michael, 1964—
Owls / by Michael George.
p.   cm.
Includes index.
Summary: Simple questions and answers introduce the physical
characteristics, behavior, habitat, and life cycle of owls.
ISBN 1-56766-481-4 (lib. bdg. : alk. paper)
1. Owls—Juvenile literature.
[1. Owls—Miscellanea. 2. Questions and answers.]   I Title.
QL696.S8G462   1998
598.9'7—dc21   97-28749
CIP
AC

Photo Credits

© 1993 Alan G. Nelson/Dembinsky Photo Assoc. Inc.: 10
© 1991 Alan G. Nelson/Dembinsky Photo Assoc. Inc.: 9, 19
© 1992 Anthony Mercieca/Dembinsky Photo Assoc. Inc.: 16
© 1996 Anthony Mercieca/Dembinsky Photo Assoc. Inc.: 6
© Art Wolfe/Tony Stone Images: 26
© David E. Myers/Tony Stone Images: 2
© David N. Davis: 30
© 1997 J. Shaluta, Jr./Dembinsky Photo Assoc. Inc.: 23
© 1997 Joe Sroka/Dembinsky Photo Assoc. Inc.: 15
© John Warden/Tony Stone Images: 24
© Robert and Linda Mitchell: 20
© 1993 Rod Planck/Dembinsky Photo Assoc. Inc.: 13
© 1991 Sharon Cummings/Dembinsky Photo Assoc. Inc.: 29
© Tim Davis/Tony Stone Images: cover

On the cover...

Front cover: This *great horned owl* is sitting in a pine tree.
Page 2: This *spotted owl* is resting on a branch.

Table of Contents

Do you think of owls as large, evil birds swooping out of the sky on Halloween night? Maybe a witch on a broomstick is following close behind! Or perhaps you think of the wise old owl, giving advice with a thoughtful stare.

These images are shared by many people, but none of them is actually true. Owls are not evil creatures that hang out with witches. Nor are they wiser than robins, sparrows, or any other bird. However, the truth about owls is just as fascinating as the stories.

⇐ This spotted owl is watching for its next meal.

What Do Owls Look Like?

Owls look different from all other birds. They have round faces covered with soft, fluffy feathers. Their faces are outlined by two large circles called **facial disks**. Owls have big, round eyes. They also have sharp, curved beaks called **bills**.

These *saw-whet owls* are sitting on a pine branch. ⇒

There are about 140 different kinds of owls. Some owls are small, but others are huge. *Eagle owls* are the largest of all. They have six-foot **wingspans**. A wingspan is the distance from one wing tip to the other. But not all owls are giants. Some kinds, like *screech owls*, are not much bigger than other birds.

Where Do Owls Live?

Owls live in almost every country of the world. They are found in cold, snowy areas and in hot jungles. Some owls live on open grasslands. Others live in thick forests. Some owls even live in big cities!

Great gray owls like this one are very large. ⇒

Some owls live in very cold regions. The *snowy owl* lives in the Far North. It has a thick, warm coat of white feathers. The white feathers help the owl blend in with its snowy surroundings. This coloring protects the owl from enemies. It also helps the owl sneak up on the animals it hunts for food. The animals it hunts are called its **prey**.

This *snowy owl* blends into the surrounding snow. ⇒

Most owls live far from frozen areas. Instead of white coats, they have darker feathers to help them hide. Owls that live in thick forests usually have small bodies and short wings, too. That makes it easy for them to fly through the forest's leaves and branches.

What Are Baby Owls Like?

Unlike most other birds, owls do not build fancy nests. Most owls just add a few twigs and leaves to a hole in a tree. Others, like *burrowing owls*, build their nests underground.

Baby owls, called **owlets**, hatch from eggs in the spring. Newborn owlets do not look much like their parents. They have small wings and are covered with soft, fuzzy feathers. When the owlets are about two weeks old, adult feathers begin to replace the fuzzy ones. Soon, the mother owl teaches her babies to fly. The young owls leave their parents when they are a few months old.

These *long-eared owlets* are very fluffy. ⇒

Where Do Owls Go During the Day?

People and other animals rarely see owls, even though some owls are quite large. Most owls are active at night and sleep during the day. They often sit close to tree trunks, on high branches. This resting place is called a **perch**. The owls' feathers blend in with the trees, making them very hard to see.

← This *eastern screech owl* is watching for small animals.

How Do Owls See and Hear?

Most other birds' eyes face to the sides, but an owl's eyes face straight ahead. The owl must turn its head to see something to its side. Luckily, owls' necks bend and twist easily. An owl can turn its head so far that it can see backwards. Sometimes it looks as if its head can spin all the way around! Owls also have very good eyesight. They can even see in the dark.

This *barn owl* is turning its head while it watches things. ⇒

Many owls have long feathers that stick up on top of their heads. These feathers are called **ear tufts**. They are not really on the owl's ears, though. The owl's ears are hidden beneath its feathers. Owls have excellent hearing.

How Do Owls Hunt?

Owls use their sharp hearing and eyesight to hunt for food. Most owls eat insects, mice, birds, or snakes. Some large owls also hunt squirrels, rabbits, and even young deer.

Most owls hunt only at night. The owl sits on a tree branch, watching and listening. When it spots something to eat, the owl swoops down from its perch. Soft feathers on the owl's wings help it fly very quietly. In an instant, the owl is on top of its prey. It spreads its sharp claws, called **talons**, and snatches up its meal.

How Do Owls Eat?

After catching its dinner, the owl carries it back to its perch. Owls do not have teeth, so they cannot chew their food. They must swallow their prey whole—even the bones! If the meal is too big, the owl tears it into pieces with its sharp bill.

This barn owl has just caught a tasty mouse to eat. ⇒

People do not need to be afraid of owls. In fact, we should be happy that they are around. Owls hunt mice and other pests that might otherwise bother us. They also are very beautiful animals. So the next time you are in the woods at night, listen for an owl—"WHOO! WHOO!" Maybe if you hoot back, it will answer!

Glossary

bills (BILLZ)
An owl's bill is its sharp beak. Owls use their bills to tear their food into pieces.

ear tufts (EER TUFTS)
Ear tufts are long feathers that stick up on many owls' heads. Ear tufts are not actually on the owl's ears.

facial disks (FAY–shul DISKS)
Facial disks are the large circles that outline an owl's face.

owlets (OW–lets)
An owlet is a baby owl. Very young owlets have soft, fluffy feathers.

perch (PERCH)
A perch is a place where an owl rests. Owls also like to eat at their perch.

prey (PRAY)
Prey are animals that are hunted for food. Prey for an owl includes mice and other small animals.

talons (TA–lunz)
Talons are the sharp claws on an owl's foot. Owls use their talons to grab and hold on to food.

wingspans (WING–spanz)
A wingspan is the distance from one wing tip to the other. Some owls have very large wingspans.

Index